Lan Fɔ Rid Ɛn Rayt Krio

Esme James

First Edition. Published 2024

ISBN: 9798332378218

Editors: Yvonne Thompson-Kponou

Sa Lon Krio (SLK) Limited

This book is dedicated to all Krio speakers who wish to become literate in Krio, so that they can read and write the language.

It is also dedicated to all teachers and students of the Krio language.

Table of Contents

Acknowledgements

Putting this book together has been extremely rewarding, especially since it is the product of a team effort from three continents. Thanks go to:

Ronald Johnson who first set out to put together lessons and exercises in Krio as an aid to teaching speakers of the language how to read and write it. His efforts served as the groundwork that went into making this publication possible.

Malcolm Finney, Linguistic Professor at California State University in Long Beach for his scholarly guidance on the linguistics of the Krio language.

Raymond Johnson, Chairman of the Board of Sa Lon Krio who advised and assisted with hours of research.

Emmenette Mason and Florence Johnson for their invaluable insights on the content and structure of the book.

Foreword

In the mid-nineties, the Government of Sierra Leone introduced the teaching of five local languages, including Krio, into the Junior Secondary School curriculum. This was a welcome move within educational circles. Krio, the lingua franca of Sierra Leone, is spoken throughout the country.

What continues to be the greatest challenge, however, is that Krio is largely a spoken language and most of its speakers can neither read nor write it. So, in spite of the initial high interest, the actual teaching and learning of Krio began to wane because there were not enough teachers trained to teach the language to meet the standards set by the West African Examinations Council (WAEC), for the Basic Education Certificate Examination (BECE) taken by pupils after a three-year course. This has led to dwindling numbers of candidates and the performance of those who have been taking the exam over the past decade has continued to decline.

In spite of this, however, Sierra Leoneans both at home and in the diaspora continue to show interest in the need to have reading and writing Krio taught and learnt correctly.

Over the past thirty years many authors, following in the footsteps of the iconic Krio-English Dictionary compiled by Clifford Fyle and Eldred Durosimi Jones (1980), have produced material suitable for use in schools and for those wishing to learn to read and write Krio.

Sa Lon Krio is adding another resource with this first volume of five lessons, that will help both native and foreign speakers to read and write Krio well. These lessons target fluent Krio and English speakers who want to learn to read and write Krio.

Yvonne Thompson-Kponou

August 2024

Introduction

Krio is fundamentally an English-based creole language comprising English and West African languages.

The lessons in this book set out to draw the key differences between the English and Krio alphabets and, in particular, their similarities and peculiarities.

The Krio alphabet comprises the English consonants (except q and x), all of the English vowels, and adds symbols for one Krio consonant (ŋ) and two Krio vowels (ɛ and ɔ).

Since the Krio alphabet is phonetic, many words directly adopted from English are spelt quite differently.

Other differences such as the very infrequent use of double letters and the lack of silent letters in Krio are discussed.

The Krio Phonetic Alphabet

These lessons describe and make use of the phonetic system used in reading and writing Krio. It is important to note the unique letters associated with intrinsic Krio vowel sounds and a few consonants and sounds that differ from the standard English ones.

The technique of reading and writing Krio phonetically is introduced. In cases where Krio has directly adopted an English word, the Krio phonetic alphabet is used to spell the word.

The phonetic approach makes learning to read and write the language easier than English since only a few simple rules are required to spell the words in the language.

At the end of these lessons, you should be conversant with the consonants and vowels of the Krio alphabet and their correct sounds and symbols. Oral, visual and written repetition of the word examples given would accelerate assimilation and retention of the spelling of words, and proper use of the vowels in particular.

Phonetics

Phonetics is a system of writing having a direct correspondence between symbols and sounds. Krio uses a phonetic alphabet based on the international phonetic alphabet. This means:

- Each Krio letter has a fixed and unique phonetic sound that does not vary, irrespective of where it occurs in a word or sentence.
- Krio is read phonetically that is, each Krio word is the vocal combination of the unique sounds of the individual letters.
- Krio is written by combining the unique sounds of the individual letters and transcribing them to spell words.

Developing your skills of using the Krio phonetic alphabet would assist you to read and write the language and attain proficiency within a short time.

Many Krio words and names are derived directly from the English language. When writing in Krio, the phonetic alphabet and system is used to spell Krio words and English words adopted into the language.

The Krio and English Alphabets

Consonants

English Consonants	b	c	d	f	g	h	j	k	l	m	n		p	q	r	s	t	v	w	x	y	z
Krio Consonants	b	c	d	f	g	h	j	k	l	m	n	ŋ	p		r	s	t	v	w		y	z
Krio Variants		k,s												kw						ks		

Where Krio and English have the same consonants as shown above, they have the same or similar sounds.

In this book, Krio letters are identified by the characters between bars as in |a| whereas English letters are identified by characters between curly braces as in {a}.

Where English may have multiple pronunciations for the same consonant, Krio only has one. For example, in English the {g} in gate is pronounced differently from the {g} in danger. Krio always uses the |g| in gate and uses |j| when spelling danger (*denja*).

In Krio, the consonants (letters) {q} and {x} do not exist. **Krio sound equivalents** for these letters are |kw| for {q} and |ks| for {x} as shown in the table on page 13.

The Krio consonant |c| is only used in combination with the letter **h** to form |ch|. In all other cases, |c| is replaced by |k| or by |s|.

The Krio consonant |ŋ| is used to represent the nasal {ng} sound in English.

Vowels

In Krio there are seven vowels as opposed to English that has only five. These are shown in the table below.

English Vowels	a	e		i	o		u
Krio Vowels	a	e	ɛ	i	o	ɔ	u

The seven Krio vowels are different from the five English vowels in many *visual* and **sound** respects, so you need to pay special attention to them.

The vowels in common differ in that the Krio versions are pronounced in only one way, whereas in English, each vowel has multiple pronunciations and sometimes, are not pronounced at all.

Some pronunciations of English vowels are replaced by two-letter combinations that mimic the English sound. For example, the {i} in the English word 'hide' is replaced by the two-letter combination |ay| to give the Krio spelling 'ayd'.

Many readers get confused by the new Krio letters and think that there are many more than the three (ɛ, ɔ, ŋ) we are introducing in this book. Another area of confusion is the fact that the phonetic nature of the Krio alphabet tends to result in shorter words compared to the English language (e.g. '*laf*' vs. 'laugh' or '*futbɔl*' vs 'football'). Diligent study and practice will overcome these barriers in a very short time.

Krio Has No Silent Letters

Many words in English have one or more letters (consonants or vowels) that are not pronounced. For example, most English words that end with {e} such as "bone", "phone" and "time" are pronounced with the {e} silent. However, in Krio, the |e| at the end of words is always pronounced. For example, the Krio word for the English 'today' is '*tide*' and it is pronounced 'ti-de'. This can be confusing for first time readers of Krio since a Krio word may look like an English word but is pronounced differently and has a different meaning.

Krio Uses Double Letters Infrequently

Many words in English have same sound double consonants or double vowels or both.

Examples:

Apple, syllabus, apparel --------- (double consonants)

Steer, feeble, book --------------------- (double vowels)

Football, balloon --- (double consonants and vowels)

With very few exceptions, Krio does not use double letters. When they do occur (for example, *waala*), each letter is pronounced separately. The Krio spelling of the English words with double letters is usually with the equivalent single Krio letter. For example, the double consonants ({ss}, {pp}, {rr} and {tt}) in the English words 'pass', 'apple', 'marry' and 'matter' are replaced by the single Krio letter equivalent consonants (|s|, |p|, |r| and |t|) to give *'pas', 'apul', 'mared' and 'mata'* respectively. Similarly, the double vowels ({ee} and {oo}) in 'meet', 'foot', and 'book', are replaced by (|i| and |u|) to give *'mit, 'fut', and 'buk'.*

English and Krio Vowel Combinations

Many English vowel combinations are represented by a single vowel in Krio. For example, the sound of 'ea' (as in bead, or head) is represented by |i| (*bid*) or |ɛ| (*ɛd*) in Krio based on the phonetic sound. Similarly, the sound of {ou} (as in loud) is represented in Krio by |aw| (*lawd*). The sound of {i} (as in high) is represented in Krio by |ay| (*ay*).

Guide to Phonetic Reading and Writing of Krio

Step 1. Your aim is to become conversant with both the **visual and sound attributes** of all the letters of the phonetic Krio alphabet together with applying specific rules used in reading and writing the language. These lessons will guide you through the process.

Step 2. Consonants. Most of the Krio and English consonants **look** and **sound** the same. You are already familiar with most of them. Some English consonant combinations would be replaced by the phonetic Krio consonant (e.g. laugh becomes *laf* and tough becomes *tɔf*).

Step 3. Vowels. The seven Krio vowels are different from the five English vowels in many **visual** and **sound** respects, so you need to pay special attention to them.

Step 4. Reading and Writing

The key is to have a full appreciation of the phonetic [unique letter sound] composition of each word in both reading and writing it. Initially, you should say each word aloud (whether reading or writing), to develop your skills in this area.

Words could be broken down into small phonetic modules. The module can be a single word or as small as a single letter. For example, the word cham (chew) is a single phonetic module |**cham**|. The word mɛmba (member) has the two syllables |**mɛm-ba**|. Similarly, the word arata (rat) can be progressively read and written as |**a-ra-ta**|.

Once you have identified this modular breakdown, it is important in all cases that all the phonetic sounds and symbols (letters) are always pronounced and written correctly. This technique is particularly useful for long words that look unfamiliar when written down at first.

Peculiarities in Krio of consonants, vowels and sounds will be highlighted under relevant headings.

Summary

Consonants

1. Krio and English consonants generally sound the same
2. In Krio, the sound of each letter never changes
3. Krio uses |c| only when it is followed by |h| |ch|; otherwise use |k| or |s|
4. Krio uses |kw| for English {q} and |ks| for English {x}
5. Krio does not use double consonants. Double letters in English (e.g. ({ll}, {rr}, {ss}) are replaced by the single letter Krio equivalent (|l|, |r|, |s|).

Vowels

6. Krio does not have any double vowels, except in very few instances. The English double vowels ({ee}, {oo}), are replaced by the phonetic Krio vowels (|i|, |u|).
7. English vowel combinations are replaced by the equivalent Krio phonetic vowel. Some English vowel sounds are replaced by Krio combinations.

Phonetics

8. The Krio phonetic alphabet is used to read and write the language.

9. Krio does not have any silent letters. Each letter or group of letters in Krio has a distinct sound and is always pronounced.

10. Many English vowel combinations are represented by a single vowel in Krio based on the phonetic sound. In some cases, English vowel combinations or sounds of single vowels are represented by Krio letter combinations.

Chapter 1:   The Vowels |a| and |e|

English Vowels	a	e		i	o		u
Krio Vowels	a	e	ɛ	i	o	ɔ	u

Scope. This Chapter covers the use of the two Krio vowels |a| and |e|. Krio words are spelt using these vowels and the Krio consonants. Examples are given of words using only one of these two vowels and words that use both vowels. Use of these vowels is compared to English words that have the same sound but are spelt differently.

Goal. At the end of this lesson, you should be conversant with the correct sounds and images of the two Krio vowels |a| and |e| and be able to use them to spell Krio words. Oral, visual and written repetition of the examples given would accelerate assimilation and retention of the words, and of the vowels in particular. For this lesson, we shall use words with only the Krio vowels |a| and |e|.

Krio Vowel |a|

The letter {a} in English can have different pronunciations, but the pronunciation of |a| in Krio is always as the {a} in the English words: mat, pass, fast, cat and rat. Any English words adopted into Krio with the sound of |a| (e.g. laugh or farm) are spelt with |a| in Krio (e.g. *laf* or *fam*).

Krio Vowel |a| Word Examples

Krio	English
Bat	Bat
Tam	Term
Las	Last
Was	Wash
Pan	Pan
Fat	Fat
Wata	Water
Pas	Past
Laf	Laugh
Afta	After

Krio Vowel |e|

In English, {e} can have different pronunciations or not pronounced at all. In Krio, the pronunciation of |e| is always as the {a} in the English words: ale, able, table, pale, gate and fate. Any English words with the sound of |e| (e.g. rain or eight) are spelt with |e| in Krio (e.g. *ren* or *et*).

Krio Vowel |e| Word Examples

Krio	English
Met	Mate
Ret	Rate
Vel	Veil
Get	Gate
Mek	Make
Tek	Take
Be	Bay
Me	May
Gem	Game
Plet	Plate
Yes	Ear
Wet	Wait, White

Word Examples Using Both |a| and |e|

Krio	English
Denja	Danger
Mared	Marriage
Deta	Data
Sela	Sailor
Fawe	Far away
Edat	Headache
Sefa	Safer
Egen	Again

Word Practice

The following Krio words contain only the vowels |a| and |e| and are intended to help with familiarisation in the reading and writing of these vowels. Reading the words aloud several times while focusing on the vowels would assist the memory process in both the reading and writing modes. You should practise the reading and writing tips given on pages 18-19. You are also encouraged to select and spell your own Krio words for further practice.

as	arata	banana	fana	anch	pan
dat	mama	papa	wach	famyad	gad
fan	baf	chaj	waf	plaba	tranga
pach	vab	baba	yad	asma	chans
pata	fala	kat	langa	granat	dans

fa	kalbas	bakyad	lafta	kanda	plasas
dak	staga	wachman	afta	lamp	chak
beg	bek	eg	tek	pe	nel
men	mel	bren	chen	brev	tres

spes	gens	nem	wep	es	gret
sem	mekes	wek	fet	mek	grev
pe	kes	les	red	ven	tret
bandej	greta	neba	pared	chenj	agens
reza	wetman	pej	saten	setan	manej

Summary

Krio Vowels |a| and |e|

1. The Krio |a| <u>always</u> sounds as the {a} in English papa, mama, mat or cat.

2. The Krio |e| <u>always</u> sounds as the {a} in English able, table, gate, pale and fate.

3. Adopted English words that pronounce the letters {a} and {e} differently are spelt with the Krio phonetic equivalents.

Chapter 2:   The vowels |ɛ|, |i| and |o|

English Vowels	a	e		i	o		u
Krio Vowels	a	e	ɛ	i	o	ɔ	u

Scope. This chapter covers the use of the three Krio vowels |ɛ|, |i| and |o|. Krio words are spelt using these vowels and the Krio consonants. Examples are given of words using one or more of these vowels as well as the two vowels, |a| and |e|, covered in Chapter 1.

Goal. At the end of this lesson, you should be familiar with the correct sounds and typefaces of the three new vowels and be able to use them correctly to spell Krio words, using the phonetic guidance given in the Introduction. You should pay particular attention to all vowels since you are already familiar with the sounds, typefaces and use of the consonants.

Krio Vowel |ɛ|

The pronunciation of the Krio letter |ɛ| is always as the {e} in the English words: help, sell, melt and felt. Any adopted English words with the sound of |ɛ| (e.g. health or sweat) are spelt with |ɛ| in Krio (e.g. *ɛlt* or *swɛt*).

Krio Vowel |ɛ| Word Examples

Krio	English
Ɛni	Any
Bɛtɛ	Better
Dɛm	Them
Pɛtɛtɛ	Potato
Lɛta	Letter
Bɛt	Bet
Bɛn	Bend
Twɛlv	Twelve
Fɛt	Fight
Gɛt	Get
Rɛd	Red

Krio Vowel |i|

In English, {i} can be pronounced differently in different words. In Krio, the pronunciation of |i| is always as the {i} in the English words: sit, till, fit and dim.

Any adopted English words with letter combinations that sound like |i| (e.g. beat, party) are spelt with |i| in Krio to give (*bit, pati*).

Krio Vowel |i| Word Examples

Krio	English
Titi	Girl
Pikin	Child
Api	Happy
Pati	Party
Pit	Spit
Tik	Stick
Tif	Steal
Tit	Teeth
Fiva	Fever
Tikit	Ticket
Makit	Market
Ziro	Zero

Krio Vowel |o|

In English, {o} can be pronounced differently in different words, but the pronunciation of |o| in Krio is always as the {o} in the English words: go, mow, so and mode.

Any adopted English words with letter combinations that sound like |o| (e.g. coat, load) are spelt with |o| in Krio.

Krio Vowel |o| Word Examples

Krio	English
Got	Goat
Bot	Boat
Kol	Coal
Lod	Load
Soba	Sober
Rod	Road
Bon	Bone
Ol	Old
Moto	Motor
Po	Poor

Word Practice

The Krio words below containing the |ɛ|, |i| and |o|
vowels are intended to help with familiarisation in the
reading and writing of these vowels. Read the words
aloud several times, noting the phonetic combinations,
while focusing on the vowels. This would assist the
memory process in both the reading and writing modes.
You are also encouraged to select and spell your own
words for further practice.

yɛri	lɛs	gɛst	rɛst	drɛb	dɛf
mɛtal	trɛnk	bɛl	kɛr	rɛklɛs	nekɛd
fɛnfɛn	lɛkɛ	gɛda	ɛva	pɛdal	brɛkfas
mɛsej	tɛmpa	fɛnch	sɛnta	jɛs	vɛst
ejɛnt	wɛdin	ɛniwe	lɛta	ɛvride	lɛnt

lisin	rizin	skias	kwik	pila	sink
angri	pink	bizi	gladi	fri	wida
pisis	jiraf	bia	siti	mi	klia

apia	nia	shia	biabia	wip	riva
ebi	bita	wida	karozin	sip	polis

brok	spok	tot	moto	bod	ston
sote	wok	fol	bonga	vot	rop
pok	blo	rol	kongosa	fon	kot
broko	gost	to	kondo	nansitori	obiata
poltri	lokal	notis	smoka	soshial	lɛsin
pɛtrol	wikɛnd	jɛntri	tɛnki	wisɛf	sistɛm

Summary

Krio Vowels |ɛ|, |i| and |o|

1. Krio |ɛ| <u>always</u> sounds as the {e} in English help, self, fresh and get.
2. Krio |i| <u>always</u> sounds as the {i} in English pin, fit, limp and lip.
3. Krio |o| <u>always</u> sounds as the {oa} in English goat, boat, float and goal.
4. English words that contain letter combinations that sound like |ɛ|, |i| and |o|, are spelt with those letters in the equivalent Krio words.
5. Together with the vowels covered in Chapter 1, you should now be familiar with the sounds, typefaces and use of the five Krio vowels: |a| |e| |ɛ| |i| |o|

Chapter 3:   The vowels |ɔ| and |u|

English Vowels	a	e		i	o		u
Krio Vowels	a	e	ε	i	o	ɔ	u

Scope. This Chapter covers the use of the final two Krio vowels: |ɔ| and |u|. The spellings of Krio words using these vowels and the consonants are provided. Several examples are given of words using one or both of these vowels and all the other vowels covered in Chapters 1 & 2.

Goal. At the end of this lesson, you should be conversant with the correct sounds, typefaces and usage of all the seven vowels of the Krio alphabet and be able to use them correctly to spell words, using the phonetic guidance given in the Introduction. You should pay particular attention to all vowels since you are already familiar with the sounds, typefaces and use of the consonants.

Krio Vowel |ɔ|

The pronunciation of the Krio vowel |ɔ| is as the {or} in the English words or, mortal, organ and order.

Phonetic Note

Any adopted English words with letter combinations that sound like |ɔ| (e.g. chalk, awful, rough) are spelt with |ɔ| in Krio (*chɔk, ɔful, rɔf*).

Examples:

Krio	English
Ɔda	Order & Other
Pɔt	Port & Pot
Pɔta	Porter
Kɔba	Cover
Bɔta	Butter
Plɔt	Plot
Ɔrinch	Orange (fruit)
Ɔrenj	Orange (colour)
Bɔdi	Body
Pikchɔ	Picture
Tɔf	Tough

Krio Vowel |u|

The pronunciation of |u| is as the {u} in blue, flute, put and salute.

|u| is also used for the English double vowels 'oo' in words such as pool, broom and room, whose Krio spellings are *pul*, *brum* and *rum* respectively.

Phonetic Note

The Krio word |yu| sounds like and means the same as the English word 'you'. However, it also represents the {u} sound in English-based words such as sal**yu**t rɛg**yu**la, pop**yu**la, **yu**man and amb**yu**lans. Contrast these words with the sound of |u| in uman, ustɛm and rum.

Many English words ending in {le} (e.g. table, ankle) are spelt phonetically in Krio by the replacing the {le} with |ul| based on the pronunciation of the word to give (tebul, ankul).

Examples

Krio	English
Fut	Foot
Grɔmbul	Grumble
Gyambul	Gamble
But	Boot
Ful	Full & Fool
Fyu	Few
Bɔtul	Bottle
Lus	Loose
Rut	Root
Nyu	New
Ɔnkul	Uncle
Kitul	Kettle
Angul	Angle
Simpul	Simple
Taytul	Title

Word Practice

The Krio words below containing the |ɔ| and |u| vowels are intended to help with familiarisation in the reading and writing of these vowels.

Read the words aloud several times, noting the phonetic combinations, while focusing on the vowels. This would assist the memory process in both the reading and writing modes. You are also encouraged to select and spell your own words for further practice.

wori	dɔg	mɔs	blɔf	kɔtin	fɔls
prɔmis	trɔs	nɔs	stɔdi	blɔk	nɔlɛj
bɔmp	jɔni	mɔt	pɔvati	lɔyal	tɔpik
Gɔd	frɔnt	dɔti	ashɔbi	gɔspɛl	kɔba
fɔtin	bɔbɔ	nɔmba	ɔda	bɔbɔ	fɔrɛst

fɔni	mɔnin	drɔp	tɔrɔ	pɔsin	trɔki
drɔm	drɔ	bɔbul	wɔdrob	jɔngul	siriɔs
fulɔp	rumɔ	trɔbul	pɔsibul	bɔndul	tumɔs
dɔbul	rikɔd	ɔlrɛdi	jisnɔ	sɔspɛkt	ɔgfut
ɔpozit	agyu	pɛbul	rɛgyula	vɔlɔntia	rɔba

lut	wud	shuga	fufu	luz	fufu
skru	pruv	sutebul	jus	luk	yuman
fukfuk	gud	butu	brum	yu	fulman
bush	tumbu	push	wund	muf	gumbe
rut	shub	buk	mun	pus	tumbu
vyu	yuniti	egugu	slipul	shub	yuba

Summary

Krio Vowels |ɔ| and |u|

1. Krio |ɔ| <u>always</u> sounds as the {or} in English port, sort, ought and bought.

2. Krio |u| <u>always</u> sounds as the {u} in English put, bull, and as the {oo} in room, foot and boot.

3. Together with Chapters 1 & 2, you should now be familiar with all seven of the Krio vowels below:

$$|a| \quad |e| \quad |ɛ| \quad |i| \quad |o| \quad |ɔ| \quad |u|$$

Phonetics

4. The Krio word |**yu**| means the same as the English word 'you'. |**yu**| also represents the {u} sound in some English-based words such as rɛg**yu**la.

5. Any adopted English words with letter combinations that sound like |ɔ| are spelt with the letter |ɔ| in Krio.

6. Many English words that end in {le} are phonetically pronounced as |ul| in Krio (e.g kettle becomes *kitul*).

Chapter 4:   Review of Krio Spelling

Scope. This Chapter is a revision of the contents of Chapters 1, 2 & 3. The previous lessons covered usage of all the seven Krio vowels which form a very important element of learning to read and write Krio.

Examples of Krio words are given using the vowels and consonants while making reference to the phonetic information contained in the Introduction.

An outline of mnemonics is given to assist further in information storage and retrieval.

Goal. At the end of this lesson, you should be able to readily identify the correct written symbols and sounds of all vowels and consonants and be able to use them correctly to spell the majority of Krio words.

Review of the Krio Alphabet

Consonants

	b	c	d	f	g	h	j	k	l	m	n		p	q	r	s	t	v	w	x	y	z
English Consonants	b	c	d	f	g	h	j	k	l	m	n		p	q	r	s	t	v	w	x	y	z
Krio Consonants	b	c	d	f	g	h	j	k	l	m	n	ŋ	p		r	s	t	v	w		y	z
Krio Variants		k,s												kw						ks		

The Krio and English consonants shown above have the same typefaces and sounds.

The Krio consonants do not have the letters {q} and {x}. **Krio sound equivalents** for these letters are |kw| for {q} and |ks| for {x} as shown. Use of these equivalents will be covered in Chapter 5.

The Krio consonant |c| is only used in combination with the letter |h| to form |ch|. In all other cases, {c} is replaced by |k| or |s|. These attributes would be developed further in Chapter 5.

The Krio consonant |ŋ| is used to represent the |ng| sound in English.

Vowels

English has only five vowels whereas Krio uses a total of seven vowels.

English Vowels	a	e		i	o		u
Krio Vowels	a	e	ɛ	i	o	ɔ	u

The pronunciation of |a| is as the {a} in the English words: afar, pass, cat and rat.

The pronunciation of |e| is as the {a} in the English words: ale, able and table.

The pronunciation of |ɛ| is as the {e} in the English words: help, self and met.

The pronunciation of |i| is as the {i} in the English words: it, fill and river.

The pronunciation of |o| is as the {o} in the English words: go, boat and mow.

The pronunciation of |ɔ| is as the {or} in the English words: for, more and tore.

The pronunciation of |u| is as the {u} in the English words put, blue and lute. |u| is also used as the double vowel {oo} in the English words boot, room and tool.

You should review all the Krio vowels and become thoroughly conversant with them in sound, sight and usage. The section on Mnemonics below could help with remembering any vowels you are still having problems with.

Krio Uses Double Letters Infrequently

While English has many words with double consonants and or double vowels, almost no Krio words have same sound double consonants or double vowels.

Examples

English	English Type	Krio
Apple	Double consonants	Apul
Book	Double vowels	Buk
Football	Double consonants and vowels	Futbɔl

Examples

English	Krio
Pass	Pas
Beggar	Begaman
Earring	Yerin
Glass	Glas
Possible	Pɔsibul

Mnemonics

Mnemonics is a memory technique that aids storage of information in, and retrieval from, the brain. This is done by associating what you want to remember with objects, ideas or words you are familiar with. The strongest mnemonics are formed with concrete nouns; that is, nouns that can be identified by sight, touch, feel, hearing or smell.

For example, if you want to remember the colours of the rainbow [red, orange, yellow, green, blue, indigo and violet] in the correct order, a suitable mnemonic is: **R**ain **O**n **Y**our **G**arden **B**rings **I**ncreased **V**egetation. A mnemonic for the Krio version [rɛd, ɔrenj, yala, grin, blu, indigo ɛn vayolɛt] could be: Rɛd Ɔrinch Yala Gwɛva Brakɛt Insay Vas.

Similarly, the following are examples of mnemonics for the seven Krio vowels:

As	Erima	ɛnta,	Iyamide	opin	ɔda	buk
a	e	ɛ	i	o	ɔ	u

Apul	eg	ɛn	ivin	ogi,	ɔl na	fud
a	e	ɛ	i	o	ɔ	u

You need only *one* mnemonic for **one topic or idea** you want to remember. If you are having problems remembering any of the vowels, you may find any **one** of the following mnemonics helpful:

|a| na fɔ **apul**

|e| na fɔ **ebul**

|ɛ| na fɔ **ɛlifant**

|i| na fɔ **Iyamide**

|o| na fɔ **Olu**

|ɔ| na fɔ **ɔrinch**

|u| na fɔ **uman**

Alternatively, you can form your own mnemonics.

Further Guide to the Use of Phonetics in Krio

Let us review the principles of phonetic reading and writing Krio outlined in Chapter 1.

Each Krio letter has a fixed and unique phonetic sound that does not vary, irrespective of where in a word or sentence it occurs.

Krio is read phonetically, that is, each Krio word is the vocal combination of the unique sounds of the individual letters.

Krio is written by combining the unique sounds of the individual letters and transcribing them to spell words.

It was noted in Chapter 1 that in both reading and writing, breaking words down to manageable phonetic modules is particularly useful for long and unfamiliar Krio words.

Krio has adopted many words from English with the same meaning and similar pronunciation. In the table on page 51, the Krio and English words sound the same, but the Krio words are visually different because of the application of the unique, Krio phonetic alphabet.

Study each word in the table by first saying the syllables of the English word **[column 1]** aloud but slowly, while noting the corresponding Krio phonetic modules **[column 2]**. Joining the modules gives the complete Krio word **[column 3]**.

Similarly, to write a Krio word, break down the **sound** of the word into convenient phonetic modules **[as in column 2]** that you can spell readily. Joining the modules would give you the spelling of the full word **[as in column 3]**.

Examples

English	Krio Phonetic Modules	Krio
Education	Ɛd-yu-ke-shɔn	Ɛdyukeshɔn
Invitation	In-vi-te-shɔn	Inviteshɔn
International	In-ta-na-shɔn-al	Intanashɔnal
Peninsular	Pɛ-nin-syu-la	Pɛninsyula
Comfortable	Kɔm-fɔt-e-bul	Kɔmfɔtebul
Computer	Kɔm-pyu-ta	Kɔmpyuta
Keyboard	Ki-bɔd	Kibɔd
Secondary	Sɛ-kɔn-da-ri	Sɛkɔndari
Recommendation	Rɛ-kɔm-ɛnd-e-shɔn	Rɛkɔmɛndeshɔn
Application	Ap-li-ke-shɔn	Aplikeshɔn
Prescription	Pri-skrip-shɔn	Priskripshɔn
Refreshment	Ri-frɛsh-mɛnt	Rifrɛshmɛnt

Word Practice

The Krio words below containing all the seven vowels are intended to help with familiarisation in the reading and writing of these vowels. Some of the words may seem unfamiliar but if you read the words aloud several times, noting the phonetic combinations, while focusing on the vowels, you will recognize all of them. This will assist the memory process in both the reading and writing modes.

You are also encouraged to select and spell your own Krio words for further practice.

Alafia	ambɔg	ashɔbi	absɛnt	agyu	anbag
akara	banguls	baranta	biznɛs	bɔlɔbɔlɔ	bɔtin
bumbu	blant	bred	brij	butu	blɔf
domɔt	daknɛs	dɔbul	ebul	ebi	bɔks

bikɔs	biskit	chakman	chikin	chekere
chakra	chukchuk	dans	dɛbul	pisful

ejɛnt	ɛlɛba	ɛmti	ɛvritɛm	fiaful
prea	renbo	rensizin	rɛjista	rɛklɛs
inlɔ	jakas	jakato	jublɔks	jok

rɔnbɛlɛ	shabi	sɔktit	stori	shɛgurɛ
flag	fiba	femɔs	finga	fɔl
fridɔm	fɔtin	gara	injɛkshɔn	gɔt
gumbe	gris	grap	grepfrut	igen
gɔrila	irɛgyula	impruv	introdyus	ivin

klas	kasada	kapinta	kach	kitul
krabit	kres	lapa	lɛda	likwid
lukinglas	lɛpɛt	masta	milɛ	milk
sampul	siriɔs	snek	wokman	tɛnki

mɔnki	mɔndɔ	mɔdan	yɛstade	nachɔral
nebul	notis	nia	trade	obiata
opin	ovin	ɔnɛs	ɔmbrɛla	ɔnkul
ɔndastand	pasivia	peshɛnt	prɛd	trɛd

uswan	tumara	twis	tyun	uspat
zip	vab	vanish	viniga	vatikal
waka	wantɛm	wekin	wɛda	wisɛf
zibra	yanda	yams	yabas	yanga

Sɔnde	Mɔnde	Tyusde	Wɛnsde	Tɔsde
Frayde	Satide	Jɛnyuari	Fɛbyuari	Mach
Epril	Me	Jun	Julay	Ɔgɔst
Sɛptɛmba	Ɔktoba	Novɛmba	Disɛmba	nyu-ia

Summary

Mnemonics

1. Just as in English, the technique of mnemonics can be used to come up with phrases or sentences in Krio that can remind you of the pronunciation of vowels.

Phonetics

2. Krio has adopted many words from English with the same meaning and similar pronunciation. You can spell these words using the unique, Krio phonetic alphabet to represent the sounds made in pronouncing the words.

3. When writing unfamiliar words, identify the syllables and spell each syllable using the Krio phonetic alphabet.

Chapter 5: Krio Letter Combinations

Scope. This Chapter deals with specific letter combinations used in Krio to produce certain sounds. Examples are given of words with these combinations.

Goal. At the end of this lesson, you should be able to recognize readily the special letter combinations and use them correctly.

Consonants

English Consonants	b	c	d	f	g	h	j	k	l	m	n		p	q	r	s	t	v	w	x	y	z
Krio Consonants	b	c	d	f	g	h	j	k	l	m	n	ŋ	p			r	s	t	v	w		y	z
Krio Variants		k,s												kw							ks		

Vowels

English Vowels	a	e		i	o		u
Krio Vowels	a	e	ɛ	i	o	ɔ	u

Specific Letter Combinations and Usage

All the letter combinations covered in this section are fixed in spelling, pronunciation and usage; they never vary.

1. **Krio Letters |c|, |ch|, |k| and |s|**

    |c| is never used on its own. It is always used in combination with |h| to form |ch| which is pronounced as the {ch} in chap, batch and match.

    Where a word starts with {c} that sounds like an |s|, **Krio** uses the letter |s|.

    |k| is used as an equivalent for {c} in all other cases.

Examples of words using these combinations are given in the table on page 58.

Examples

Combination	Krio	English
|ch|	Ticha	Teacher
	Chɔch	Church
	Kichin	Kitchen
	Chip	Cheap
	Chif	Chief
	Wich	Witch
	Bich	Beach
|k| used for {c}	Klɔk	Clock
	Kyaful	Careful
	Chakol	Charcoal
	Kabej	Cabbage
	Kyandul	Candle
	Koknat	Coconut
|s| used for {c}	Sinima	Cinema
	Silin	Ceiling
	Sɛnta	Center
	Sakul	Circle
	Simɛnt	Cement
	Siti	City
	Risiv	Receive

2. Krio Letter Combinations |kw|, |ks| and |ng|

Krio uses |**kw**| as an equivalent sound for English letter {**q**}. For example, the word 'question' becomes *kwɛshɔn* or *kwɛstyɔn* and 'quick' becomes *kwik*.

Krio uses |**ks**| (and for a few words |**gz**|) as an equivalent sound for English letter {**x**}.

Krio uses |**ŋ**| as an equivalent sound for English {**ng**}.

Examples of words using these combinations are given in the table on page 60.

Examples

Combination	Krio	English
|kw| used for {q}	Kwin	Queen
	Kwik	Quick
	Kwata	Quarter
	Kwɛshɔn	Question
	Kweri	Query
|ks| used for {x}	Aks	Ask & Axe
	Bɔks	Box
	Sɔksid	Succeed
	Ɛkspɛkt	Expect
	Siks	Six
|gz| used for {x}	Ɛgzakt	Exact
	Ɛgzam	Exam
	Ɛgzampul	Example
	Ɛgzɔst	Exhaust
|ŋ| used for {ng}	Tɔŋ	Town, Tongue
	Dɔŋ	Down
	Lɔŋ	Long
	Lɔŋtɛm	Long ago
	Kiŋ	King
	Siŋ	Sing
	Fritɔŋ	Freetown

3. Krio Letter Combinations |aw|, |ay| and |ɔy|

|Aw|, |ay| and **|ɔy|** are fixed letter combinations used for fixed Krio sounds.

Krio uses **|aw|** as the {ow} in cow, now, and frown; and as the {ou} in noun, pound, proud and sound.

Krio uses **|ay|** as the {i} in die, fight, light and bright.

Krio uses **|ɔy|** as the {oi} in coil, soil, boil and spoil.

Examples of words using these combinations are given in the table on page 62.

Mnemonic Tips

The following mnemonics might help you remember the sounds of these letter combinations

|aw| na fɔ **aw**tsayd

|ay| na fɔ **Ay**ɔ

|ɔy| na fɔ **ɔy**l

Examples

Combination	Krio	English
|aw|	Aw	How
	Brawn	Brown
	Sawnd	Sound
	Prawd	Proud
	Rawnd	Round
	Klawd	Cloud
	Frawn	Frown
|ay|	Tray	Try
	Yay	Eye
	Lay	Lie
	Nayntin	Nineteen
	Dayamɔn	Diamond
	Prayz	Prize
|ɔy|	Bɔy	Boy
	Kɔyl	Coil
	Jɔy	Joy
	Vɔys	Voice
	Ɔysta	Oyster

4. Krio Letter Combinations |gb|, |kp|, |ny| & |zh|

There are many Krio words that use the |gb|, |kp| and |ny| special combinations. The |zh| combination is also used in a few Krio words.

Examples

Combination	Krio	English
|gb|	Yagba	Busyness
	Gbana	Difficult
	Gbakanda	Bold
	Gbosgbos	Confusion
|kp|	Kpakɔ	Back of head
	Akpata	Large, flat stone
	Kpatakpata	Completely
	Ɔkpɔlɔ	Frog
|ny|	Nyanga	Flamboyant
	Nyuzpepa	Newspaper
	Nyusans	Nuisance
|zh|	Plɛzhɔ	Pleasure
	Mɛzhɔ	Measure
	Trɛzhɔ	Treasure

Word Practice

The following Krio words contain the special letter combinations covered earlier and are only intended to help with familiarisation in the reading and writing of these vowels. Reading the words several times while focusing on the special combination will assist the memory process in both the reading and writing modes. If the words seem unfamiliar, try saying them with different inflections and emphasis.

You are also encouraged to select and spell your own Krio words for further practice.

chɔch	ayɔn	blay	kam	klas	miks
sɔks	fayn	tray	kwaya	lɔyal	kakroch
flay	gawn	wayn	pawda	sɛmitri	yɔŋuman
kan	kalbas	aydul	krawo	usay	satisfay

siksti	rayt	ɛkspɛl	sayz	tayp	kamp
rayd	dɔŋ	yawo	sayn	lawd	kaw
aksidɛnt	maynd	fakay	mikschɔ	chɔklet	chupit
bɔtaflay	kray	siŋ	awtrayt	gayd	kwis

doks	lay	rikwaya	laybri	tawzin
siment	oyl	niksnaks	komot	junio
odoyo	taya	akshon	fray	brayt
shayn	insay	midwayf	pawa	nildon

wayd	krawd	kom	noyzi	kweri
plekech	noys	kad	chia	layf
layon	toylet	nayn	fayl	layt
brin	naw	kawad	aydia	poyzin

English and Krio Words

First time readers of Krio who have been educated using the English language have to distinguish carefully between English and Krio words. Those words which look, sound and have the same meaning in both Krio and English should cause no problems. Some examples of such words include Banana, Bush, Gold, Land, Chin, Spirit and Finish.

Krio words that do not look like, sound like and have a different meaning from English words are easy to read with very little confusion. So, after a little practice, you should have no problems with Krio words like *baranta*, *akara* and *krabit* which originate from African languages.

The areas of most confusion are words that are spelt like English words but are pronounced differently and may have completely different meanings. If you study the table below very closely, you can see that:

- The English word 'we' is spelt '*wi*' in Krio.
- The English word 'way' is spelt '*we*' in Krio.
- And the English word 'why' is spelt '*way*' in Krio

English	Krio
We	Wi
Way	We
Why	Way
Buy	Bay
Die	Day
Day	De
Wait	Wet

Summary

The Krio consonant |c| is only used in combination with the letter |h| to form |ch|. In all other cases, {c} is replaced by |k|, or by |s| in certain words.

The Krio consonants do not have the letters {q} and {x}. Krio sound equivalents for these letters are |kw| for {q} and |ks| (and for a few words |gz|) for {x}.

Krio uses |ŋ| as an equivalent sound for nasal {ng} sound in English.

|Aw|, |ay| and |ɔy| are fixed letter combinations used for fixed Krio sounds.

Many Krio words use the special letter combinations of |gb|, |kp|, |ny| and |zh|. Other combinations that are used include |sh| and |th|.

Conclusion

The lessons in this booklet are meant as a short and simple introduction to the reading and writing of the Krio language using the standard Krio alphabet.

The three new Krio letters (ɛ, ɔ, ŋ) have been introduced and explained, removing all confusion as to their sound, meaning and usage. The key differences between the English and Krio phonetic alphabets are described and many other areas of confusion have been addressed.

Future volumes will provide guidance on more advanced reading and writing skills. More details can be found on our website **www.salonkrio.com**.

These lessons should also enable early Krio readers to read the story book: ***Krio Nansi Stori Dɛm*** which contains some Krio folktales with their translations into English. The Krio stories serve as good exercises in reading Krio prose.

Made in United States
Orlando, FL
30 September 2024

52109400R00039